W9-BVS-535

ESSENTIAL ELEMENTS

FOR STRINGS

A COMPREHENSIVE STRING METHOD

By
Michael Allen • Robert Gillespie • Pamela Tellejohn Hayes
Arrangements by John Higgins

Congratulations! You have made one of the most important decisions in your life by joining the orchestra. The key to succeeding with *Essential Elements For Strings* is your commitment to daily practice. Each time you learn a new note, count a new rhythm, or play a melody with a friend, you become a more accomplished musician. We are thrilled to welcome you to our orchestra family, and wish you the very best for a lifetime of musical success.

OF THE CELLO

The string family includes the violin, viola, violoncello, and the double bass. The early ancestors of the string family were the Arabian rebab and rebec, popular during the 14th-16th centuries. During the 1500's, there were two types of viols: the viola da gamba, played on the knee, and the viola da braccia, played on the shoulder.

The sound of the violoncello, called 'cello' for short, is pitched an octave below the viola. The cello has a warm tone and is capable of playing a wide range of dynamics. It is often referred to as the tenor of the orchestra. Antonio Stradivari, and the Guarneri and Guadagnini families were famous instrument makers from the 17th and 18th centuries, and their cellos are still in use today.

Nearly every composer has written music for the cello, including Johann Sebastian Bach, Ludwig van Beethoven, and Peter Illyich Tchaikovsky. Famous cello performers include Janos Starker, Leonard Rose, Pablo Casals, and Yo Yo Ma.

ISBN 0-7935-4305-3

HAL•LEONARD®
CORPORATION
7777 W. BLUEMOUND RD. P.O. BOX 13819 MILWAUKEE, WI 53213

04619003

THE CELLO

Scroll
Pegs
Peg box
Nut

Fingerboard

Neck

Upper bout

"C" bout

f hole

Bridge

Sound post
(inside)

Fine tuners

Tailpiece

End pin

String instruments are delicate. Follow your teacher's guidelines in caring for your instrument, and it will last forever.

- Follow your teacher's instructions when removing the instrument and bow from the case.

- Protect your instrument from heat, cold, and quick changes in temperature.

- Always wipe off the instrument with a soft dry cloth. Be sure to remove all fingerprints and rosin.

Accessories
- Rosin

- Soft cloth

- Rock stop

THE BOW

Tip   Stick   Winding   Adjusting screw

Bow hair   Ferrule   Frog

- Never touch the bow hair.

Instrument provided courtesy of Scherl & Roth and United Musical Instruments U.S.A., Inc.

BASIC SKILLS

The best way to learn your instrument is to practice one skill at a time. Repeat each step until you are comfortable demonstrating it for your teacher and classmates.

Step 1 - Remove the bow from the case and put it in a safe place. Open the case and remove the cello. Identify all parts of the cello.

Step 2 - Adjust the length of the end pin so that the scroll of the cello is near your nose when standing.

Step 3 - Sit on the front half of your chair with your feet positioned underneath your knees. Place the end pin directly in front of you one arm's length away.

Step 4 - Lean the cello slightly to the left and allow the instrument to rest against your chest. The 'C' peg should be near your head behind your left ear, and both knees should touch the cello just below the 'C' bout. It may be necessary to readjust the length or position of the end pin. Identify the letter names of each string: C (lowest pitch), G, D, A. Raise your right index finger over the strings and pluck them as directed by your teacher. Plucking the strings is called *pizzicato*, and is abbreviated *pizz*.

Step 2

Step 3

Step 4

Beat = The *Pulse* of Music

The beat in music should be very steady, just like your pulse.

Music Staff

The music staff has 5 lines and 4 spaces.

Bar Lines and Measures

Bar lines divide the music staff into measures. The measures on this page have four beats each.

Quarter Note

♩ = 1 Beat of Sound

Notes tell us how high or low to play, and how long to play.

Quarter Rest

𝄽 = 1 Beat of Silence

Rests tell us to count silent beats.

1. LET'S PLAY "OPEN D"

Open string.

pizzicato (pizz.) ◄ Pluck the strings.

2. LET'S PLAY "OPEN A"

pizz.

Keep a steady beat.

3. TWO'S A TEAM

pizz.

4. AT PIERROT'S DOOR   Your teacher will play the melody while you play this part.

pizz.

Bass Clef

Clefs indicate a set of note names.

Time Signature (Meter)

$\frac{4}{4}$ — 4 beats per measure

$\frac{4}{4}$ — ♩ or 𝄽 get one beat

The time signature tells us how many beats are in each measure *and* what kind of note gets one beat.

Double Bar

A double bar indicates the end of a piece of music.

Counting

Count 1 & 2 & 3 & 4 &
Tap   ↓ ↑ ↓ ↑ ↓ ↑ ↓ ↑

One beat = Tap toe **down** on the number and **up** on "&." Always count when playing or resting.

5. COUNT THE BEAT   Identify the clef and time signature before playing.

6. MIX 'EM UP

Repeat Sign

Go back to the beginning and play the music again.

7. COUNT CAREFULLY   Write in the counting before you play.

8. ESSENTIAL ELEMENTS QUIZ   Keep a steady beat when playing or resting.

SHAPING THE LEFT HAND

Step 1 - Shape the left hand as shown.
Be certain your palm faces you.

D STRING NOTES

```
0 = open string
1 = 1st finger
2 = 2nd finger
3 = 3rd finger
4 = 4th finger
```

Step 2 - Bring your left hand to the fingerboard.
Place your fingers on the D string, keeping your
hand shaped as shown below. Be sure your thumb
is behind the second finger and slightly bent.

G is played with 4 fingers on the D string.

F♯ is played with 3 fingers on the D string.

E is played with 1 finger on the D string.

Listening Skills   Play what your teacher plays. Listen carefully.

9. LET'S READ "G"   Say or sing the note names before you play.

Sharp ♯   A sharp raises the sound of notes and remains in effect for the entire
measure. Notes without sharps are called **natural** notes.

10. LET'S READ "F♯" (F-sharp)

▲ Play all F♯'s. Sharps apply to the entire measure.

11. LIFT OFF   Say or sing the note names before you play.

Count   1 & 2 & 3 & 4 &   1 & 2 & 3 & 4 &   1 & 2 & 3 & 4 &   1 & 2 & 3 & 4 &

12. ON THE TRAIL

13. LET'S READ "E" Remember to count.

14. WALKING SONG

15. BELGRADE SQUARE

16. ICE DANCING

17. ROLLING ALONG

Go to next line. ▼

18. ESSENTIAL ELEMENTS QUIZ Keep a steady beat.

Work-outs

Pencil Hold

Step 1 - Hold a pencil in your left hand about waist level.

Step 2 - Place the tip of your right thumb between the first and second joints of your second finger.

Step 3 - Place the pencil between your thumb and 2nd finger, while keeping your thumb gently curved.

Step 4 - The pencil should touch your first three fingers between the first and second joints, and touch the fourth finger at the first joint, as shown.

Step 5 - Remove your left hand from the pencil. Keep your fingers relaxed. Practice shaping your hand on the pencil until it feels natural to you.

Pencil Hold

Pencil Hold Exercises

I'm Out Of Here
Wave good-bye while keeping your wrist relaxed.

Thumb Flexers
Flex your thumb in and out.

Knuckle Turnovers
Turn your hand over and be sure your thumb knuckle is bent, as shown.

Fourth Finger Taps
Tap your fourth finger.

First Finger Taps
Tap your first finger.

Elbow Energy
- Swing your right elbow away from your body.
- Open your right forearm, as shown.
- Close your right forearm.
- Swing your elbow back toward your body.

Knuckle Turnovers

Elbow Energy

Folk songs have been an important part of cultures for centuries and have been passed on from generation to generation. Folk song melodies help define the sound of a culture or region. This folk song comes from the Slavic region of eastern Europe.

19. MORNING DANCE

Slavic Folk Song

20. AN "A" FOR THE DAY

▲ Keep fingers down when you see this bracket.

21. GOOD KING WENCESLAS

Welsh Folk Song

22. TUNNELS

▲ Form a "tunnel" over the A string with your fingers in playing position.

23. SEMINOLE CHANT

24. LIGHTLY ROW

▲ Prepare F♯ before playing.

A STRING NOTES

D is played with 4 fingers on the A string.

C♯ is played with 3 fingers on the A string.

B is played with 1 finger on the A string.

Listening Skills

Play what your teacher plays. Listen carefully.

Ledger Lines

◄ Ledger Lines

◄ Ledger Lines

Ledger lines extend the music staff higher or lower.

25. LET'S READ "D"

26. LET'S READ "C♯" (C-sharp)

▲ Play all C♯'s. Sharps apply to the entire measure.

27. LIFT OFF

28. CARIBBEAN ISLAND

Review Pencil Exercises on page 8 daily.

29. OLYMPIC HIGH JUMP

30. LET'S READ "B"

31. HALF WAY DOWN

32. RIGHT BACK UP

 Scale   A scale is a sequence of notes in ascending or descending order.

33. DOWN THE D SCALE

34. ESSENTIAL ELEMENTS QUIZ - UP THE D SCALE

35. SONG FOR CHRISTINE

36. COUNTING CHALLENGE

Work-outs

Left Hand Exercises

Finger Taps
Tap fingertips on any string.
Practice in different combinations of fingers.

Strummin' Along
Strum the strings with your 4th finger while swinging your elbow.

Holding The Bow

Step 1 - Identify all parts of the bow (see page 2). Hold the bow in your left hand near the tip with the frog pointing to the right.

Step 2 - Place the bow between your right thumb and 2nd finger. The tip of your thumb will contact the stick next to the frog, and your 2nd finger will extend to the ferrule.

Step 3 - Shape the remaining fingers on the bow stick as shown.

Step 4 - Turn your right hand over, and be sure your thumb is curved.

Step 5 - Hold the bow and repeat the exercises on page 8.

Note Names

Music is normally written without the note name on the inside.
For example:

Note Names   **D**   **E**   **F♯**   **G**   **A**   **B**   **C♯**   **D**

Memorize these note names.

37. CAROLINA BREEZE   Say or sing the note names before you play.

38. JINGLE BELLS   J.S. Pierpont

39. OLD MACDONALD HAD A FARM   American Folk Song

Austrian composer **Wolfgang Amadeus Mozart** (1756-1791) was a child prodigy who first performed in concert at age 6. He lived during the time of the American Revolution (1775-1783). Mozart's music is melodic and imaginative. He wrote hundreds of compositions, including a piano piece based on this familiar song.

40. A MOZART MELODY

Adapted by W.A. Mozart

Key Signature D MAJOR

A key signature tells us what notes to play with sharps and flats throughout the entire piece. Play all F's as **F♯** (F-sharp) and all C's as **C♯** (C-sharp) when you see this key signature, which is called "D Major."

41. MATTHEW'S MARCH

▲ Play F♯'s and C♯'s when you see this key signature.

42. CHRISTOPHER'S TUNE

43. ESSENTIAL ELEMENTS QUIZ - WHAT'S FOR DINNER? Write the note names below.

Note Names: ___ ___ ___ ___ ___ ___ S M ___ ___ ___ ___ ___ ___ ___ ___ ___ ___ !

Continue reviewing the exercises on page 8 daily with the bow.

Theory — Harmony

Harmony is two or more different pitches sounding at the same time. A **duet** is a composition for two players. Practice this duet with a friend, and listen to the harmony. Throughout this book, **A** = Melody and **B** = Harmony.

44. LONDON BRIDGE - Duet Say or sing the note names before you play.

English Folk Song

Work-outs — Shadow Bowing

Shadow bowing is bowing without the instrument. One way to shadow bow is to bow on the rosin.

Step 1 - Tighten the bow hair as instructed by your teacher.

Step 2 - Place the rosin in your left hand. Hold the bow in your right hand.

Step 3 - Shadow bow by slowly moving the bow back and forth on the rosin. Be sure to move the bow, not the rosin.

Down Bow ⊓ Move the bow away from your body (to the right).

Up Bow V Move the bow toward your body (to the left).

45. ROSIN RAP #1 Bow these exercises on the rosin.

46. ROSIN RAP #2

47. ROSIN RAP #3

LET'S BOW _____

Regular Bow Hold

Thumb Placement

 Play what your teacher plays. Listen carefully.

48. BOW ON THE D STRING

arco ◄ Play with the bow on the string.

49. BOW ON THE A STRING

String Levels Your whole arm moves when bowing on different strings. Memorize these guidelines:

- Move your arm foward and up to play **higher**-pitched strings.
- Move your arm back and down to play **lower**-pitched strings.

50. RAISE AND LOWER

51. TEETER TOTTER

52. MIRROR IMAGE

Bow Lift , Lift the bow and return to its starting point.

53. A STRAND OF D 'N' A

54. ESSENTIAL ELEMENTS QUIZ - OLYMPIC CHALLENGE

Echoes Echo fingered note patterns with your bow on the string, as played by your teacher.

Alert: Before turning the page, practice playing notes from the D scale while bowing.

PUTTING IT ALL TOGETHER

Congratulations! You are now ready to practice like an advanced player by combining left and right hand skills while reading notes. Follow these steps for success:

Step 1 - Tap your toe and say or sing the letter names.
Step 2 - Play *pizz.* and say or sing the letter names.
Step 3 - Shadow bow and say or sing the letter names.
Step 4 - Bow and play as written.

55. BOWING "G"

56. BACK AND FORTH

57. DOWN AND UP

58. NON-STOP FLIGHT

59. BOWING "D"

60. LITTLE STEPS

61. ELEVATOR DOWN

62. ELEVATOR UP

63. AVALANCHE

64. TRIBAL LAMENT

65. NAME THIS TUNE

66. ESSENTIAL ELEMENTS QUIZ - GRANDPARENT'S DAY

American Folk Song

1st and 2nd Endings

Play the 1st ending the 1st time through. Then, repeat the same section of music, skip the 1st ending, and play the 2nd ending.

67. FOR PETE'S SAKE

Tempo Markings Tempo markings tell us the speed of the music. Tempo markings are usually written in Italian and appear above the staff.

Andante = Slow, walking tempo   **Moderato** = Moderate tempo   **Allegro** = Fast, bright tempo

68. LIGHTLY ROW - Orchestra Arrangement

Arr. John Higgins

A = Melody. **B** = Harmony. The cellos will usually play part B in the orchestra.

69. JOLLY OLD ST. NICHOLAS - Orchestra Arrangement

Arr. John Higgins

SPECIAL CELLO EXERCISE

While the basses learn a new note, draw the bar lines in the music below. Then write in the counting.

70. LET'S READ "C#" - Review

 Folk songs often tell stories. This **Israeli folk song** describes a game played with a dreidel, a small table-top spinning toy that has been enjoyed by families for centuries. The game is especially popular in December around the time of Hanukkah.

71. DREIDEL

Israeli Folk Song

Eighth Notes

72. RHYTHM RAP

73. PEPPERONI PIZZA   Shadow bow and count before playing.

74. D MAJOR SCALE   Shadow bow and count before playing.

75. BUCKEYE SALUTE

Moderato

76. ESSENTIAL ELEMENTS QUIZ

77. COTTON COUNTRY

American Folk Song

Time Signature (Meter)
$\frac{2}{4}$ - 2 beats per measure
$\frac{2}{4}$ - ♩ or 𝄽 gets one beat

Conducting   Practice conducting the two-beat pattern to feel this new pulse.

78. RHYTHM RAP

79. COUNTING TWOS

80. RECYCLABLE CANS

French composer **Jacques Offenbach** (1819-1880) played the cello and composed many works for musical theatre. One of his most famous pieces is the "Can-Can" dance from *Orpheus and the Underworld*. This popular work was written in 1858, just three years before the start of the American Civil War (1861-1865).

81. CAN-CAN - Orchestra Arrangement

Jacques Offenbach
Arr. John Higgins

Half Note 𝅗𝅥 = 2 Beats of Sound   **Half Rest** ▬ = 2 Beats of Silence

1 & 2 &

𝄽 𝄽 = ▬

82. RHYTHM RAP

83. AT PIERROT'S DOOR

French Folk Song

Moderato

Repeat Sign — Repeat the section of music enclosed by the repeat sign.

84. MICHAEL ROW THE BOAT ASHORE

American Folk Song

Moderato

85. TEXAS TWO-STRING

Pizz. this exercise with your **left hand 4th finger.** 4+ = 4th finger *pizz.*

86. FOUR BY FOUR

arco

87. 4th FINGER MARATHON

 German composer **Ludwig van Beethoven** (1770-1827) was one of the world's greatest composers. He was completely deaf by 1802. Although he could not hear music like we do, he could "hear" it in his mind. The theme of his final Symphony (No. 9) is called "Ode To Joy," and was written to the text of a poem by Johann von Schiller. "Ode To Joy" was featured in concerts celebrating the reunification of Germany in 1990.

88. ODE TO JOY
Ludwig van Beethoven

89. THIS OLD MAN
American Folk Song

 German composer **Johann Sebastian Bach** (1685-1750) wrote hundreds of choral and instrumental works during the Baroque era (1600-1750). Bach was also a master teacher, organist, and famous improviser. He had 21 children, many of whom became famous composers. European immigrants began to settle in the American colonies during Bach's lifetime.

90. ESSENTIAL ELEMENTS QUIZ - MUSETTE
Johann Sebastian Bach

G STRING NOTES

C is played with 4 fingers on the G string.

B is played with 3 fingers on the G string.

A is played with 1 finger on the G string.

Listening Skills

Play what your teacher plays. Listen carefully.

New Key Signature
G MAJOR

Play all F's as F♯ (F-sharp), and C's as C♮ (C-natural).

91. LET'S READ "G"

▲ Play F♯'s and C♮'s in this key signature.

92. LET'S READ "C" (C-natural)

▲ Play C♮'s, not C♯'s, in this key signature.

93. LET'S READ "B"

94. LET'S READ "A"

95. LIFT OFF   Name the notes before you play.

Round

A round is a musical form where performers play or sing the same melody and enter at different times. This is called **counterpoint**, a type of harmony. Rounds can also be called canons. Divide into groups, and play "Scotland's Burning" as a round. When group 1 reaches the third measure, group 2 plays from the beginning, etc.

Time Signature
(Meter)

$\frac{3}{4}$ - 3 beats per measure
- ♩ or 𝄽 gets one beat

Conducting

Practice conducting this three-beat pattern.

102. RHYTHM RAP

103. COUNTING THREES

Moderato

► Move your bow slower when playing longer notes.

104. FRENCH FOLK SONG

French Folk Song

Moderato

▲ Play F♯'s and C♯'s.

 The waltz is a dance in 3/4 meter. It was first introduced in Austria during the early 1800's, about the same time as American explorers Lewis and Clark reached the Pacific Ocean. Many waltzes are still popular on today's symphony orchestra programs.

105. A GRAND WALTZ

106. ESSENTIAL ELEMENTS QUIZ - SAILOR'S SONG

English Sea Song

Allegro

Slur A slur is a curved line that connects two or more **different** pitches. Play slurred notes together in the same bow stroke.

107. STOP AND GO

108. SLURRING ALONG

109. SMOOTH SAILING

110. SLURRING ON THE G STRING

111. GLIDING BOWS

▲ Always check the key signature before you play.

112. UPSIDE DOWN

113. FRERE JACQUES - Round   Play as a round.

French Folk Song

114. D MAJOR EXERCISE

Upbeat   An upbeat is a note that comes before the first full measure.
The remaining counts are found in the last measure.

115. SONG FOR MARIA

▲ Upbeat

Where is
beat 4?

116. FOURTH FINGER D (for violins and violas)

Time Signature   **C** - Common Time   **Conducting**   Practice conducting this
(Meter)   Same as 4/4   four-beat pattern.

117. LOW DOWN

History   **Far Eastern music** comes from Malaysia, Indonesia, China and other areas. Historians believe the first orchestras, known as gamelans, existed in this region as early as the 1st century B.C. Today's gamelans include rebabs (spiked fiddles), gongs, xylophones, and a wide variety of percussion instruments. Listen to recordings of Far Eastern music and describe the sounds you hear.

118. ESSENTIAL ELEMENTS QUIZ - JINGLI NONA

Far Eastern Folk Song

Allegro

Where is
beat 4?

119. KOOKABURRA - Round

Play as a round.

Australian Folk Song

Latin American music combines the folk music from South and Central America, the Caribbean Islands, African, Spanish, and Portuguese cultures. Melodies often feature a lively accompaniment by drums, maracas, and claves. Latin American styles have become part of jazz, classical, and rock music.

D.C. al Fine

Play until you see the *D.C. al Fine.* Then, go back to the beginning and play until you see *Fine* (fee´-nay). D.C. is the abbreviation for *Da Capo,* the Italian term for "return to the beginning." *Fine* is the Italian word for "the finish."

120. BANANA BOAT SONG

Latin American Folk Song

121. FIROLIRALERA - Orchestra Arrangement

Mexican Folk Song
Arr. John Higgins

SECOND FINGER ON THE D STRING

F

is played with 2 fingers on the D string.

 Play what your teacher plays.
Listen carefully.

Natural Sign ♮ A natural sign cancels a sharp (♯) or flat (♭), and remains in effect for the entire measure.

122. LET'S READ "F" (F-natural)

 Half Step

A **half step** is the smallest distance between two notes. Listen for the half step when you go back and forth between G and F♯ while bowing. The F♯ and F♮ are a half step apart. A **whole step** equals two half steps.

123. HALF-STEPPIN' AND WHOLE STEPPIN'

1/2 step   1/2 step   Whole step   Whole step

124. NATURAL STEPS

125. HOT PASTRY

Moderato

There are no sharps in this Key Signature.

126. MINOR DETAILS

127. A-TISKET, A-TASKET

Allegro

▲ Play F♮'s and C♮'s.

128. THE SNAKE CHARMER

Andante

129. THREE IN A BOW

130. SLURRING THREES

131. THE ORIENT EXPRESS

Moderato

132. ESSENTIAL ELEMENTS QUIZ - BARCAROLLE

Jacques Offenbach

Andante

SECOND FINGER ON THE A STRING

C

is played with
2 fingers on
the A string.

 Play what your teacher plays. Listen carefully.

133. LET'S READ "C" (C-natural)

134. HALF STEP AND WHOLE STEP REVIEW

1/2 step   1/2 step   Whole step   Whole step

Theory   **Chromatics**   Chromatic notes are altered with sharps, flats, and naturals. A chromatic pattern is two or more notes in a sequence of half steps.

135. CHROMATIC MOVES

136. MELODY FOR ASHLEY

▲ Play F♮'s and C♮'s.

137. THE STETSON SPECIAL

138. BLUEBIRD'S SONG

Texas Folk Song

Africa is a large continent made up of many nations, and **African folk music** is as diverse as its many cultures. Folk songs can express feelings of love, war, sadness, or joy. This folk song is from Kenya. The words describe warriors as they prepare for battle. Listen to examples of African folk music, and describe the sound.

139. TEKELE LOMERIA
African Folk Song

140. BINGO

Where is beat 2?

141. THE BIRTHDAY SONG

Cross string smoothly

142. SNOW BOUND

 German composer **Johannes Brahms** (1833-1897) wrote four symphonies, plus many instrumental and choral works. He completed his first symphony in 1876, the same year that Alexander Graham Bell invented the telephone. This is one of the main themes, or melodies, from Brahms' *Symphony No. 1 in C minor.*

143. SYMPHONY NO. 1 THEME
Johannes Brahms

144. ESSENTIAL ELEMENTS QUIZ - MIXING FINGER PATTERNS - Round
English Round

36

Theme and Variations   Theme and Variations is a musical form where a theme, or melody, is followed by different versions of the same theme.

145. VARIATIONS ON A FAMILIAR SONG

English composer **Thomas Tallis** (1505-1585) served as royal court composer during the reigns of Henry VIII, Edward VI, Mary, and Elizabeth I. The great artist Michaelangelo painted the Sistine Chapel during Tallis' lifetime. Rounds and canons were popular forms of music during the early 16th century. Divide into groups, and play or sing the *Tallis Canon* as a 4-part round.

146. TALLIS CANON - Round

Thomas Tallis

147. FLOW GENTLY, SWEET AFTON

Welsh Folk Song

148. WABASH CANNONBALL

American Folk Song

Staccato ♩ or ♩

Staccato notes are marked with a dot above or below the note. A staccato note is played with a stopped bow stroke. Listen for a space between staccato notes.

149. PLAY STACCATO

150. MEXICAN HAT DANCE

Mexican Folk Song

Hooked Bowing

Hooked bowing is two or more notes played in the same direction with a stop between each note.

151. HOOKED ON D MAJOR

152. WALTZING BOWS

153. ESSENTIAL ELEMENTS QUIZ - POP GOES THE WEASEL

American Folk Song

C STRING NOTES

F is played with 4 fingers on the C string.

E is played with 3 fingers on the C string.

D is played with 1 finger on the C string.

Listening Skills   Play what your teacher plays. Listen carefully.

154. LET'S READ "C"

155. LET'S READ "F"

156. LET'S READ "E"

157. LET'S READ "D"

158. LIFT OFF   Name the notes before you play.

159. C MAJOR SCALE   **C MAJOR Key Signature**

All notes are naturals.

Whole Note

𝅝 ——————→ = 4 Beats of Sound

1 & 2 & 3 & 4 &
↓ ↑ ↓ ↑ ↓ ↑ ↓ ↑

Whole Rest

▬ = 4 beats of silence

| Whole Rest | ▬ | Hangs from the line. |
| Half Rest | ▬ | Sits on the line. |

160. RHYTHM RAP

Shadow Bow

Count 1 & 2 & 3 & 4 & | 1 & 2 & 3 & 4 & | 1 & 2 & 3 & 4 & | 1 & 2 & 3 & 4 &
Tap ↓ ↑ ↓ ↑ ↓ ↑ ↓ ↑ ↓ ↑ ↓ ↑ ↓ ↑ ↓ ↑ ↓ ↑ ↓ ↑ ↓ ↑ ↓ ↑ ↓ ↑ ↓ ↑ ↓ ↑ ↓ ↑

161. SLOW BOWS

Slow & 2 & 3 & 4 & | 1 & 2 & 3 & 4 & | 1 & 2 & 3 & 4 & | 1 & 2 & 3 & 4 &
Bow

Slow Bow ——————→   Slow Bow ——————→

162. LONG, LONG AGO

T.H. Baily

Moderato

Slow Bow ——→   Slow Bow ——→   Slow Bow ——→

Slow Bow ——→   Slow Bow ——————→

Theory — **Arpeggio** An arpeggio is a chord whose pitches are played one at a time. Your first arpeggio uses the 1st, 3rd, 5th, and 8th steps from the C major scale.

163. C MAJOR SCALE AND ARPEGGIO

— Arpeggio — — — — — —

164. LISTEN TO OUR SECTIONS

Violin   Viola   Cello   Bass   Vln. Vla. Vcl.   Bs.   All

165. MONDAY'S MELODY

Traditional Folk Song

Moderato

Fine

D.C. al Fine

SPECIAL CELLO EXERCISE

Write the note names below. Then, write stories using as many note names as possible.
Share your work with orchestra friends.

Team Work
Great musicians give encouragement to their fellow performers. Violin, viola, and bass players will now learn new challenging notes. The success of your orchestra depends on everyone's talent and patience. Play your best as these sections advance their musical technique.

 Play what your teacher plays. Listen carefully.

166. LET'S READ "E" - Review

167. LET'S READ "A" - Review

168. LET'S READ "G" - Review

169. LET'S READ "F♯" (F-sharp) - Review

170. LIFT OFF

171. G MAJOR SCALE IN THIRDS

Play what your teacher plays. Listen carefully.

172. LET'S READ "B" - Review

Multiple Measures Rest

Count: **1** 2 3 4 | **2** 2 3 4

The large number tells you how many measures to count and rest. Count each measure in sequence.

173. GLIDING ALONG

1 2 3 4 | **2** 2 3 4

174. G MAJOR HOOK

 Russian composer **Peter Illyich Tchaikovsky** (1840-1893) wrote six symphonies, three ballets, and hundreds of other works. He was a master at writing popular melodies. His *Symphony No. 4* was written in 1877, the same year that Thomas Edison invented the first record player, called a phonograph.

175. SYMPHONY NO. 4 THEME

Tchaikovsky

176. ESSENTIAL ELEMENTS QUIZ

42

Dynamics

Dynamics tell us what volume to play or sing.

$\boldsymbol{f}$ *(forte)*   Play loudly. Add more weight to the bow.
$\boldsymbol{p}$ *(piano)*   Play softly. Remove weight from the bow.

177. FORTE AND PIANO

178. DYNAMIC CONTRASTS

179. D MAJOR SCALE AND ARPEGGIO

$\boldsymbol{f}$-$\boldsymbol{p}$ ◄ Play *forte* the first time and *piano* the second time.

180. G MAJOR SCALE AND ARPEGGIO

181. C MAJOR SCALE AND ARPEGGIO

Austrian composer **Franz Josef Haydn** (1732-1809) wrote 104 symphonies. Many of these compositions had nicknames, including "The Surprise" *Symphony No. 94*. In the soft second movement, Haydn deliberately added sudden loud dynamics to wake up an often-sleepy audience. Play the dynamics carefully when you practice this famous theme.

Rehearsal Numbers   5   Measure numbers in squares above the staff.

182. SURPRISE SYMPHONY THEME

Franz Josef Haydn

183. CRIPPLE CREEK - Orchestra Arrangement

American Folk Song
Arr. John Higgins

Remember, **A** = Melody, **B** – Harmony (play this part in the orchestra).

184. MINUET - Orchestra Arrangement

J.S. Bach
Arr. John Higgins

Italian composer **Gioachino Rossini** (1792-1868) wrote some of the world's favorite operas. "William Tell" was Rossini's last opera, and its popular theme is still heard on television.

185. WILLIAM TELL OVERTURE - Orchestra Arrangement

Gioachino Rossini
Arr. John Higgins

186. ROCKIN' STRINGS - Orchestra Arrangement

John Higgins

187. SIMPLE GIFTS - Orchestra Arrangement

Shaker Folk Song
Arr. John Higgins

Solo

A solo is a composition written for one player, often with piano accompaniment. This solo was written by **Johann Sebastian Bach** (1685-1750). You and a piano accompanist can perform for the orchestra, your school, your family, and at other occasions. Performing for an audience is an exciting part of being involved in music.

188. MINUET NO. 2 - Solo

Johann Sebastian Bach
Arr. by John Higgins

RHYTHM REVIEW

Practice these rhythms on any pitch.

CELLO FINGERING CHART

GLOSSARY and INDEX

Essential Element	Definition
Accidental	Natural, sharp or flat not in key signature. Remains in effect for the full measure.
Allegro	Fast bright tempo. (p. 20)
Alto Clef	"C" clef used by violas.
Andante	Slow walking tempo. (p. 20)
Arco *arco*	Play with the bow on the instrument. (p. 16)
Arpeggio	A chord whose pitches are played one at a time. (p. 39)
Bach, Johann Sebastian	German composer (1685-1750). (p. 25)
Balance Point	Point on bow where weight is equally distributed.
Bar Lines	Divide the music staff into measures. (p. 4)
Bass Clef	"F" clef used by cellos and basses. (p. 5)
Beat	The pulse of music. (p. 4)
Beethoven, Ludwig van	German composer (1770-1827). (p. 25)
Bow Lift	Lift the bow and return to its starting point. (p. 17)
Brahms, Johannes	German composer (1833-1897). (p. 35)
Chromatics	Notes altered with sharps, flats, and naturals. (p. 34)
Clef	Indicates a new line of music and a set of note names. (p. 5)
Common Time	Another way to write $\frac{4}{4}$. (p. 30)
D.C. al Fine	Play until D.C. al Fine, go back to beginning, and play until you see Fine. (p. 31)
Dotted Half Note	Three beats of sound. (p. 27)
Double Bar	Indicates the end of a piece of music. (p. 5)
Down Bow	Move bow away from your body. (p. 15)
Duet	Composition for two players. (p. 15)
Dynamics	Tell us what volume to play or sing. (p. 42)
Eighth Notes	Two eighth notes = One beat of sound. (p. 22)
1st and 2nd Endings	Play the 1st ending the 1st time, skip to 2nd ending on repeat. (p. 20)
Flat	Lowers the sound of note(s) a half step.
Forte *f*	Play loudly. (p. 42)
Half Note	Two beats of sound. (p. 24)
Half Rest	Two beats of silence. (p. 24)
Half Step	Smallest distance between two notes. (p. 32)
Harmony	Two or more different pitches sounding at the same time. (p. 15)
Haydn, Franz Josef	Austrian composer (1732-1809). (p. 42)
Hooked Bowing	Two or more notes played in the same bow direction with a pause in between. (p. 37)
Interval	Distance between two notes.
Key Signature	Tells us what notes to play with sharps or flats for entire piece. (p. 14)
Ledger Lines	Extend the music staff. (p. 10)
Measure	Section of music separated by bar lines. (p. 4)

Essential Element	Definition
Moderato	Moderate tempo. (p. 20)
Mozart, Wolfgang Amadeus	Austrian composer (1756-1791). (p. 14)
Multiple Measures Rest	Tells how many measures to count and rest. (p. 41)
Music Staff	5 lines and 4 spaces. (p. 4)
Natural Sign	Cancels sharps or flats and remains in effect for the full measure. (p. 32)
Notes	Tell us how high or low to play, and how long to play. (p. 4)
Offenbach, Jacques	French composer (1819-1880). (p. 23)
Piano *p*	Play softly. (p. 42)
Pizzicato *pizz.*	Pluck the strings. (p. 3)
Quarter Note	One beat of sound. (p. 4)
Quarter Rest	One beat of silence. (p. 4)
Rehearsal Numbers	Measure numbers in squares above the staff. (p. 42)
Repeat Sign	Go back to beginning and play the music again. (p. 5)
	Repeat the section of music enclosed by the repeat sign. (p. 24)
Rests	Count silent beats. (p. 4)
Rossini, Gioachino	Italian composer (1792-1868). (p. 44)
Round	Musical form where performers play the same melody and enter at different times. (p. 27)
Scale	Sequence of notes in ascending or descending order. (p. 11)
Shadow Bowing	Bowing without the instrument. (p. 15)
Sharp	Raises the sound of note(s) a half step. (p. 6)
Solo	Performing alone or with an accompanist. (p. 46)
Slur	Curved line that connects two or more different pitches. (p. 29)
Staccato	Shortened note. Play with stopped bow stroke. (p. 37)
Tallis, Thomas	English composer (1505-1585). (p. 36)
Tchaikovsky, Peter I.	Russian composer (1840-1893). (p. 41)
Tempo Markings	Tell us the speed of music. (p. 20)
Theme and Variations	Musical form where theme is followed by variations. (p. 36)
Tie	Curved line that connects notes of the same pitch. (p. 27)
Time Signature (Meter)	Tells us how many beats per measure, and what kind of note gets one beat. (p. 5)
Treble Clef	"G" clef used by violins.
Up Bow	Move bow toward your body. (p. 15)
Upbeat	Note(s) that come before the first full measure of music. (p. 30)
Whole Note	4 beats of sound. (p. 39)
Whole Rest	4 beats of silence. (p. 39)
Whole Step	Two half steps. (p. 32)